LIFE IN A C...

Mary Draper and Jan Anderson

Contents

THOMSON

NELSON

Australia · Canada · Mexico · Singapore · Spain · United Kingdom · United States

THE AGE OF CASTLES

HUNDREDS of years ago, people needed places to live in that also protected them from their enemies. For about six hundred years, between 900AD and 1500AD, people built large stone castles across Europe and parts of Asia.

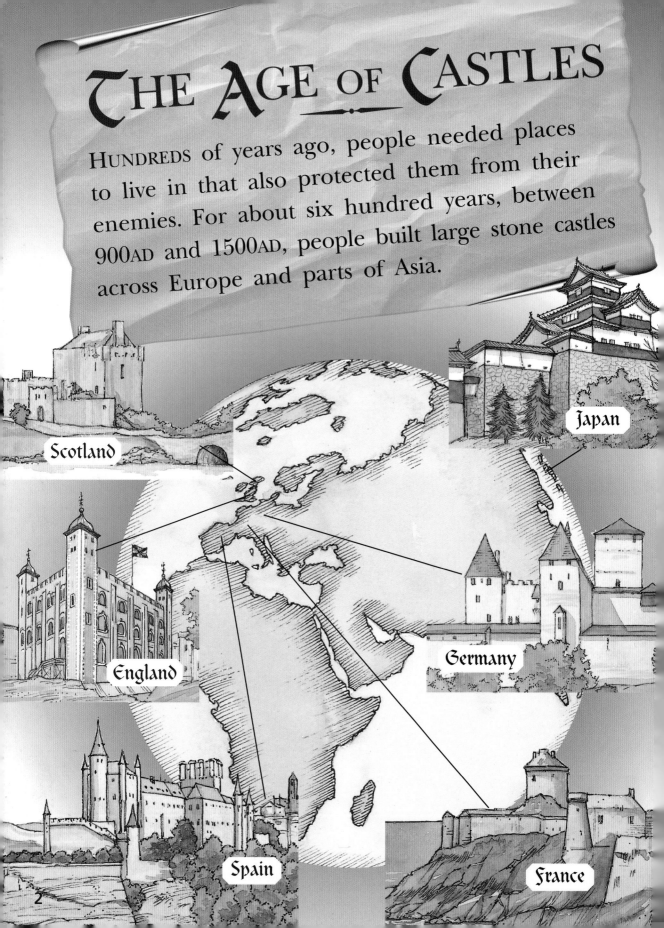

Japan

Scotland

England

Germany

Spain

France

Warwick Castle was built in England between 914AD and 1540AD.

These were rough and dangerous times, with kings, queens and **lords** fighting each other for land and power. A castle was their home, as well as their **fortress**.

The great hall of Warwick Castle.

3

BUILDING A CASTLE

WHERE a castle was built was very important. Castles built on high ground allowed people to see a long way off and all around them. They had time to prepare their defences if they saw an enemy coming.

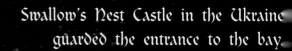

Swallow's Nest Castle in the Ukraine guarded the entrance to the bay.

Some castles were built beside rivers or ports, to protect or control **fords**, bridges or important roads and waterways. Other castles were built on the edge of cliffs, which made it easier to defend the castle and the surrounding land.

Rich and powerful landowners built large castles. Sometimes hundreds of people lived within the castle, including **nobles**, **peasants** and even whole armies. Smaller castles were built to protect just one or two families.

Hanging a large chain across the river, to stop ships sailing by, could protect a castle built on a river.

Dunnottar Castle in Scotland was built on a cliff face above the sea. This allowed the castle to be defended more easily.

The first castles were simple wooden structures. They were called 'motte-and-bailey' castles. The 'motte' was a large mound of earth, on which a **keep** was built. And the 'bailey' was a fenced area beside it. Later on, the mottes were built of stone and the keeps became bigger and stronger.

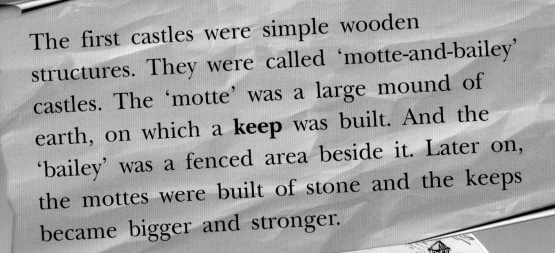

Bailey

Motte

This is a view of a typical English castle from around 1300AD.

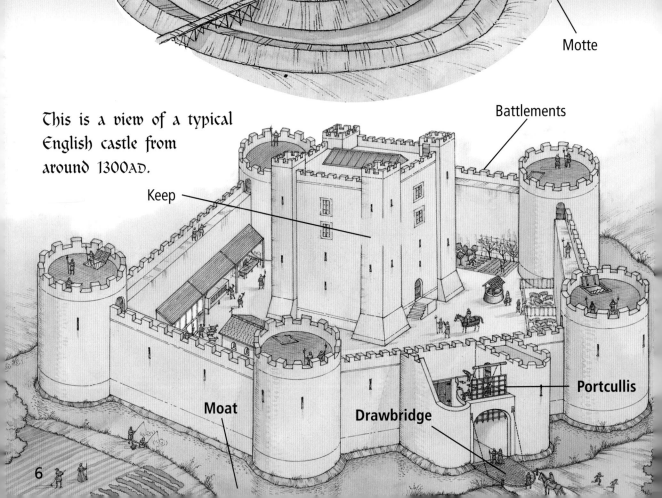

Battlements

Keep

Portcullis

Moat

Drawbridge

The first stone towers were square. They were strong but not easy to defend, as the enemy could knock the corners down.

Later, people built round towers. They had a better view of the enemy below and could try and stop the enemy from tunnelling underneath the sides of the tower.

As castles became bigger, D-shaped towers were built. A walkway went behind the tower and this made it easier for the soldiers to move themselves and their equipment around more quickly.

CASTLE LIFE

THE lord and lady, and their family and household staff, lived in the keep. This was the safest part of the castle, so visiting lords and knights also stayed there.

The lord and lady, their children and their servants all slept in the same room.

Slits in the castle walls let light into the lower levels. Rooms at the top of the castle, such as the great hall and the lord's living rooms, had bigger windows because arrows could not reach them. People living in the keep also used candles for light, but everyone else went to bed when darkness fell.

Narrow windows protected people in the lower levels of the castle from attack.

Glass was only used in the most important rooms.

Sometimes windows had shutters but no glass.

Open fireplaces were used to heat the keep. Logs, **peat** and charcoal were burned in **braziers**.

Only members of the lord's household had baths. They sat in a tub of warm water, with a curtain for privacy and warmth.

Toilets were built into the outside walls, one above the other, away from living areas. Waste fell down a chute into a ditch or pit, where it was emptied by a 'gong farmer'!

The lord controlled the land and villages surrounding the castle, and the peasants who lived there. Most of them were very poor, but they 'belonged' to the lord — they had to give a portion of everything they grew to the lord as payment for living on castle lands.

People who broke the laws could be tried before a court in the great hall of the castle and were sometimes imprisoned in the castle dungeon. Some villagers were selected for the lord's **garrison**, and trained as soldiers and archers.

The dungeon in Warwick Castle, England, was built in 1350AD.

BECOMING A KNIGHT

At six or seven years of age, the sons of noble families were sent to train as 'pages'. They served their lord meals, helped him to dress and ran messages for the family. Pages were taught to read, write and count, and also to use weapons.

When they turned fourteen, pages were ready to become 'squires'. They looked after the knights' horses and armour and practised with weapons. They helped the knights prepare for battle and often went to battle with them.

A squire became a knight when he turned 21. At a special ceremony called a 'dubbing', the squire was tapped on the shoulder with a sword and given his own **spurs** and a sword.

Knights were only allowed to fight on horseback and in hand-to-hand combat. They were expected to obey the rules of chivalry — they had to be brave, behave with honour, and protect women and weaker people.

Knights took part in **tournaments** and **jousts**, for fighting practice and entertainment. Tournaments were often very violent and lasted until one side won. In jousts, knights fought with blunted swords or **lances** until one knocked the other off his horse.

WEAPONS AND ARMOUR

DIFFERENT kinds of soldiers used different kinds of equipment to protect the lord and the castle.

A foot soldier had very little armour, except for a dagger. He wore a padded tunic and helmet, and may have been given other weapons to use such as an axe or a **halberd**.

Padded tunic

Helmets

Axe

Dagger

Halberd with axe-like blade and spike

Arrows

An archer fought with either a longbow and arrows, or a crossbow and bolts. Often he had a **buckler** to protect himself.

Pike

Longbow

Buckler

Crossbow

Bolts

A knight fought on horseback. A deep saddle and stirrups helped the knight stay firmly on the horse when he charged an enemy. He wore a tunic made of chain mail, leggings and spurs. He carried a shield, a sword and a **mace**.

The horse had to be strong enough to carry the weight of the knight, his armour and his weapons. The horse also wore armour — it had a head plate and a 'blanket' made of chain mail to protect it.

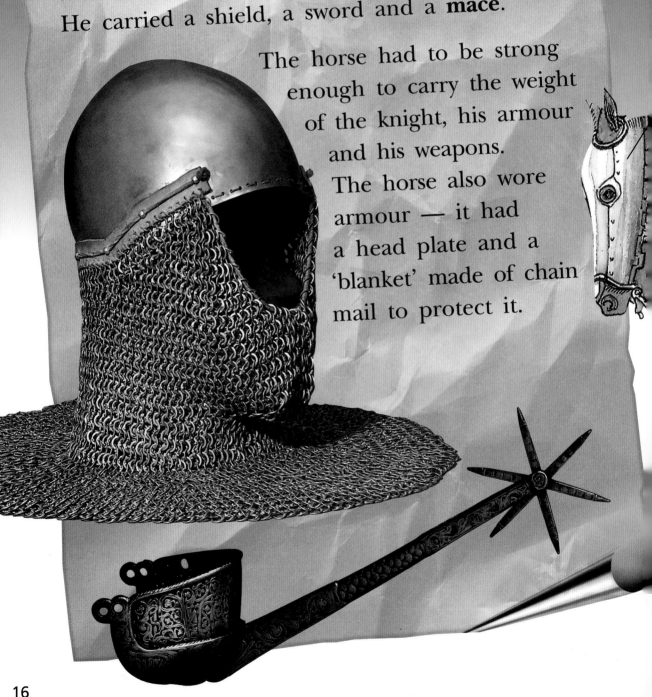

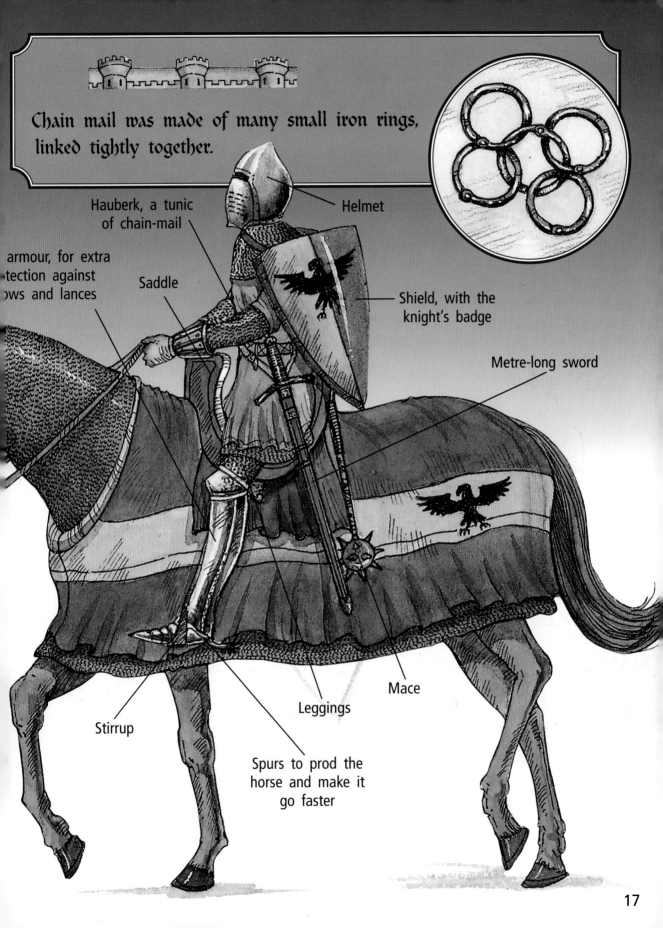

Chain mail was made of many small iron rings, linked tightly together.

Haff Hauberk, a tunic of chain-mail

Helmet

armour, for extra
...tection against
...ows and lances

Saddle

Shield, with the knight's badge

Metre-long sword

Mace

Leggings

Stirrup

Spurs to prod the horse and make it go faster

UNDER ATTACK!

Occasionally, an enemy attacked a castle and laid **siege** for months at a time. Fighting practice helped to keep the lord's armies prepared for a siege, and stores of food and arms were always kept ready for use.

During a siege, archers fired arrows from the battlements and through slits in the walls. Rocks were dropped on the enemy from above. Sometimes the knights would gallop out and make a surprise attack on the enemy outside.

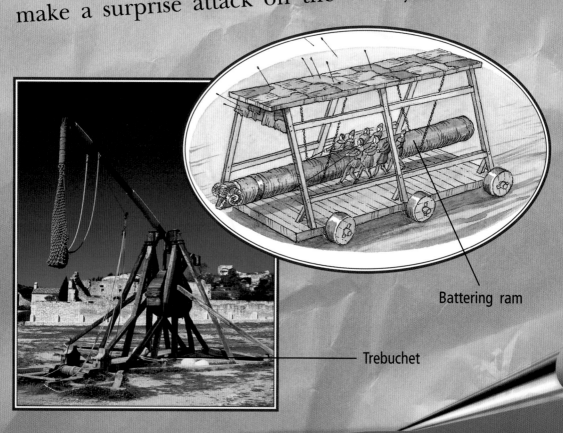

Battering ram

Trebuchet

Special machines were used to attack the castles. A **trebuchet** had a long arm that hurled rocks. A **battering ram** was a tree trunk on wheels, which was pushed against the castle gates to try and break them open.

Attackers often scaled the castle walls with ladders. Sometimes they dug tunnels under the walls, filled them with wood and set it on fire. The tunnel and wall fell in and the attackers climbed into the castle.

The attacking army camped near the castle. If the siege failed, they gave up and went away. If the defending army ran out of food or water, they had to surrender.

The rails along the bridge have been added in modern times.

Can you name the two kinds of siege engine in this picture? Pages 18 and 19 will help you.

Battlements

Defending ar

Digging a tunnel

20